MULTIPLY YOUR IMPACT

Paul Nixon and Christie Latona

Ordering Information:
Quantity sales. Special discounts are available on quantity purchases by corporations, associations, and others. For details, contact Readiness 360: 866.721.0177 or visit us online at **www.readiness360.org.**

Orders by U.S. trade bookstores and wholesalers. Please contact Fun and Done Press: (888) 879-1428 or info@funanddone.com

Printed in the United States of America

Multiply Your Impact: Making the Leap from Church Maintenance to Gospel Movement

ISBN: 978-0-9746759-3-0
Christian Leadership, Discipleship, Church Development

First Edition

Cover and Book Design by Bill Kersey, KerseyGraphics

Introduction

In this dynamic era, churches need nimble leadership: people who are *ready* to partner with God in order to maximize their impact and blessing on the world as followers of Jesus Christ. In North America, after decades of various incremental church-growth schemes, our churches are mostly shrinking (and closing). Furthermore, growth for growth's sake feels quite empty to many people in an era where society has overdosed on constant market expansion as a way toward prosperity.

> Ministry must be multiplied. The game has to change.

Anywhere in the world where we see the Christian movement thriving, the average church size may or may not be growing— but *faith communities are multiplying!* Churches with multiplication DNA do not focus on maintaining the status quo *plus a little growth to cover normal attrition.* Nor do such churches set modest growth goals for themselves as a knee-jerk response to years of decline. These churches are not focused on growing their *church business.* They are focused on making disciples to change and bless the world.

So forget church growth! In the twenty-first century, it is *multiply* or *dry up.* There doesn't seem to be another alternative.

Ministry must be multiplied. The game has to change.

We believe that any church can reclaim the foundational multiplication DNA of the Jesus movement. Unfortunately, too few leaders and churches understand what it takes and what it looks like to multiply their impact to bring more of God's reign to earth.

We hope this booklet helps you internalize the concept of multiplication so your church might move more boldly with God. We pray this boldness empowers concrete and constructive next steps that create new places of spiritual community and transformation with new people.

The eight concepts contained here are succinct. Each one builds on the other to create a culture of multiplication.

1. Understand the Multiplication Game.

2. Tend the Soil.

3. Raise the Spiritual Temperature.

4. Keep the Main Thing the Main Thing.

5. Build Positive Relationships.

6. Savor the Gift of Diversity.

7. Lead with Your Strengths.

8. Be Nimble.

Some congregations can begin the journey toward multiplication simply by incorporating these eight practices. Others may need help figuring out where they are and the steps required to journey deeper. The *Readiness 360* is a tool that any church can use to evaluate the behaviors, patterns, experiences, perceptions, and attitudes that contribute to its current capacity to step out in a bold risk-taking mission. There is no other instrument that measures church readiness for ministry multiplication like this. To learn more about this powerful tool and more resources to fuel your ability to multiply your impact, go to www.readiness360.org.

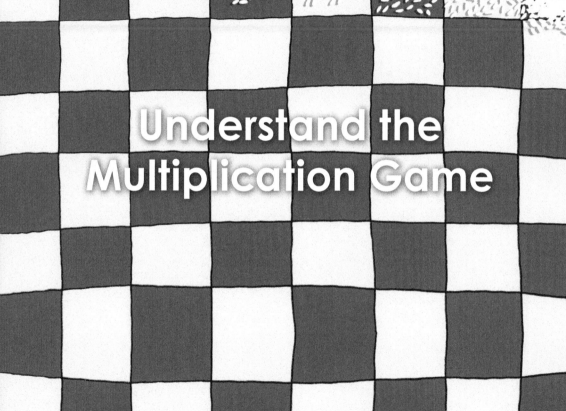

1

Understand the Multiplication Game

64

Once upon a time there was a very clever rabbit named . . . Rabbit. Rabbit invented a game called chess and went to show it to the king.

The king loved the game. He played it all day. In fact, he enjoyed it so much, he wanted to reward Rabbit.

Rabbit said no at first, but the king insisted.

So Rabbit said, "Give me some grain to eat, enough to cover my chessboard. One grain on the first square, two on the second, four on the next, and so forth, doubling the grain all the way to the 64th square."

But the king protested, "This is too little." (Forgetting that rabbits know a few things about multiplication.)

So the king's accountant began to calculate the payment. It took him two years to make the calculations. Finally he came to the king with very bad news.

"Your majesty, if we multiply one grain by two, doubling it 64 times, it is enough grain to cover the whole kingdom—indeed the whole country of India, fifty feet deep. To pay your debt to Rabbit, you would have to give away your kingdom."

But the king had another idea. He got rid of Rabbit.

However, while the accountant had been doing his math, Rabbit had been doing some multiplication of her own. With only one month's gestation, an average of eight rabbits to a litter, and four months until adulthood, 6,000 rabbits were created in the two years it took the accountant to check his figures.

When Rabbit's fate was discovered, her offspring formed an army. They overthrew the king and lived happily ever after in what became known as . . . the Kingdom of Rabbits.

Which character do you relate to the most? Which character do you wish you were more like? If you answered like most people, you'd probably want to be more like the very clever rabbit. Why? Perhaps you were taken by Rabbit's entrepreneurial gumption. Or maybe you like to back the winning team. Or possibly you have figured out—at some level—that the world belongs to those who multiply.

What does this have to do with the church?

When we've shared this story in cartoon form[1] with church leadership teams, we ask what they learned about multiplication. Generic answers usually include:

. . . What seems little ends up being significant.

. . . You don't have to start big, it just takes one (or two).

. . . You don't need to be in power to multiply.

. . . You don't need permission.

More telling answers divulge some of the dynamics that might be in play in their church setting. For example, in one of the first *Multiply Your Impact* events, one congregation said, "You'd better not wait too long to create a plan because you don't always know what else is multiplying behind the scenes."

The "second half of the chessboard" is a phrase, coined by Ray Kurzweil, to describe the point where a multiplying factor begins to have a significant economic impact on an organization's overall strategy. However, one can't get to the exponential impact of the second half of the chessboard without working the first half of the chessboard. Too often we discount the smaller products of the first multiplication events, wanting to skip to the big stuff. In the world of multiplication, you start where you are. There is no skipping ahead.

Too often we
discount the smaller
products of the
first multiplication
events, wanting to
skip to the big stuff.

Multiplication could mean many different things for a church. Sometimes new small groups, new worship communities, new hubs of activity, new people groups, new age-level ministries, new outreach initiatives, the proliferation of new ministry teams, new campuses, even new congregations that your church might help to plant.

What does multiplication mean for your church?

Multiplication also means the same things in every church:

- Leaders helping to recruit, form, and release new leaders.

- People letting go of the status quo in order to expand the church's reach and to share Christ with others.

- Thinking about the mission beyond simply caring for the folks already inside.

- Carefully evaluating everything we do in light of our stated purpose.

Are you leading, supporting or blocking the multiplication of disciples?

One surprising twist in the parable was that the rabbits multiplied over a couple years while the king's staff was diddling around. In churches that make the leap from struggling to thriving, we often see a period of time where new people get engaged and get multiplication going for a couple years before the power brokers and controllers wake up to what has happened. It is at this point that those churches complete their transformation and continue to renew and develop.

"The ingredient most necessary
to start a spontaneous movement
of God's expanding Kingdom
is found in the heart of every
follower of Christ. It is inside
of you. It is inside of me. It has
been in us all along, every one
of us who follows Christ and is
indwelt by His Spirit." —Neil Cole

 **Hop to it!**

What comes to mind when you think about multiplying your impact?

_____

_____

_____

_____

What lessons of multiplication are important for your church to understand?

_____

_____

_____

_____

2

Tend the Soil

What do you make of this?

A farmer planted seed.
As he scattered the seed, some of it fell on the road, and birds ate it.

> *[Editorial Comment: We've seen some administrative committees behave like those birds!]*

Some fell in the gravel;
it sprouted quickly but didn't put down roots,
so when the sun came up it withered just as quickly.

> *[Editorial Comment: Sometimes we take new believers and ask them to lead things before making sure they are spiritually rooted enough to sustain those things.]*

Some fell in the weeds;
as it came up, it was strangled by the weeds.

> [Editorial Comment: This can happen when we keep
> adding new ministries or values before weeding out
> those that have outlived their usefulness.]

Some fell on good earth,
And produced a harvest beyond his wildest dreams.

> [Editorial Comment: Is your congregation engaged in
> creating good earth so that God-seed might yield an
> abundant harvest?]

- An annotated version of Jesus' Parable of the Sower
(Matthew 13:3–8, The Message)

Good earth supports the following:

> . . . New and diverse leaders forming and multiplying.

> . . . Faith communities forming and multiplying.

> . . . Different styles of worship services launching and growing rapidly.

> . . . Ultimately, a great harvest.

If you look at the mountains of research conducted in the last decade across Christian denominations and cultures, you will see a vast amount of information about what propels a Christian church to thrive in a region and many "how we did it" accounts of places that have multiplied or grown. More recently, there is a focus on looking beyond simply growing one church to growing a movement. We studied much of that and discovered places of overlap. Then we went to our experience and original research to verify. Christie was project manager for the *Romans 12 Project* begun by the United Methodist General Board of Discipleship in 2007. That project went beyond the statistical data and discovered what principles were common in churches of all shapes, ages, sizes, locations, and ethnicities who were making significant—often dramatic—impacts in their communities and in the lives they touched. Paul, as a part of his role with the *Path 1* movement, did onsite research in the Far East (China, Philippines) and all over the United States (especially nondenominational contexts) to validate and witness the dynamics of ministry multiplication within the church.

> Prayer is the main strategy. Prayer is central. It is our lifeline to God.

From this we found soil elements that seem to really matter. The more of these soil boosters that are present, the more good earth you will find. In multiplying churches, we see Jesus DNA:

1. Prayer: They pray about everything. Prayer is the main strategy. Prayer is central. Prayer is not perfunctory, or a ritual performed only by a "professional." Jesus not only taught us to pray, but in the feeding of the 5,000+ he demonstrated the power of prayer, as a couple fish sandwiches became a meal for all.

2. **Abundant Evangelism:** People who encounter Jesus cannot help telling about it. This personal faith sharing tends to result in new recruits for the movement, regardless of whether the movement is theologically right, left, or center! People are constantly talking about what God is up to in their lives and/or their church. Evangelization is often focused on finding the next leaders, the people who have the gifts and/or passion. It is everyone's concern. *Never do they frame the challenge as a search for more paying customers!*

3. **Theological Simplicity:** Not to be confused with theological stupidity: this is not dumbing down the Gospel. It is just that in the churches that multiply, we find widespread consensus and clarity on the relationship between the Gospel of Jesus and God's plan for human beings. The community has managed to get its collective brain around some key truths that tie it all together. This sense of coherence empowers and gives courage to common people to dive into Scripture study themselves, without waiting for the clergy and the "experts" to show up. Jesus used his behavior and parables to make theology practical and simple.

4. **Economical Approach:** In the West, we have mastered the art of expensive church. In some contexts, we throw money at everything: from the people who serve us to the dazzling technology and buildings. However, if we are serious about multiplying our impact we need to rethink some things here. Has a materialistic distortion of "excellence in all things" replaced the value of "good enough"? Sloppiness, by definition, would not equal good enough. But neither would lavishly wasting resources on superfluous things. Think about it. There is a continuum in the economy of true excellence, and we are wise to

stay in the middle of the continuum more often than not![3] In the new places of multiplication we see a plain, functional meeting space, often leased or bartered but rarely expensive. Almost never do we see elaborate facilities with high overhead costs. And volunteers do more of the work—even some of the pastoral work! Smart economics has meant giving much of church leadership back to ordinary people.

Each one teaches one.

Jesus was essentially homeless for the three years of his active ministry. He didn't invest significant financial resources to start this movement called Christianity.

5. Trust: In churches that multiply we see trust at every level—among leaders, between leaders and followers, between clergy and laity, and in all cases, first and foremost, between people and God. Sacraments and Scripture are simply given to the people for them to steward and to use. While some uniformity is desired from place to place, that uniformity may be kept to a bare minimum, so the creativity of the people in each place can be fully unleashed. Central control is loosened, but a strong spirit of accountability

within the movement typically persists. If leaders step out of bounds with the core principles or behavioral covenants of the movement, it is addressed. But it is amazing how little leader misbehavior seems to appear in a system when there is less anxious central control. Jesus demonstrated great trust in humanity through consistently being a conduit of God's love for us.

6. **Finding and Growing Leaders:** Each one teaches one. An intentional focus on filling up the leadership pipeline and helping people discover their call and find their place in the body of Christ. This is the core flywheel of the multiplying movement! Great churches are all about developing great people to live out God's dreams in new ways. Contrast this with churches that exist to appease and please members (who behave more like consumers) or denominational overseers. Jesus sought out 12 disciples who would be leaders and poured into them.

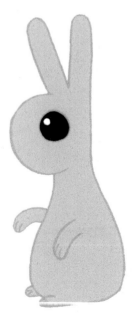

7. **High View of Scripture:** This has nothing to do
   with fundamentalism. Rather people with
   a high view of Scripture have a sense of
   expectancy that when the Word is read,
   God is in the room and is going to say
   something fresh and new to the people
   gathered and reading. Therefore the Bible
   is used easily and freely in every type of
   gathering. Laity are trusted and encour-
   aged to use it. And Scripture is consulted
   and used as an aid in times of confusion,
   debate, and learning. Jesus modeled
   this as he made reference to the Word
   of God throughout his ministry.

8. **Simple Systems:** Extremely simple local-church organization and focus (often worship, small groups, and outreach—period). Rarely do we see layers of boards and committees or complicated decision-making. This is in sync with the emerging local community-development movements that are poised to explode in the decades ahead in all arenas of life and in all cultures. In the twenty-first century, *local rules*, all the way down to the most grassroots expression of a community. This grassroots non-institutional approach mirrors the simplicity of Jesus' own ministry. He kept it simple while seeking to revive and reform the institutional church.

9. Non-Competing Priorities: Places that multiply ministry keep the main thing the main thing. Disciples making disciples trumps all other concerns. This is not to say that there aren't major disagreements. But decisions are ultimately made with the number one priority in mind. A multiplying church may explicitly limit the types of activity that it will directly sponsor—so that much is pushed to the realm of extracurricular—often encouraging members to partner with non-members for various kinds of good endeavors that are not central to the core flywheel of multiplying disciples. And such partnerships are the stuff out of which relationships (and more evangelism) are born. Nothing Jesus did was separate from or in opposition to growing disciples.

What would your church stop, start or keep doing if making disciples who made disciples was your number 1 priority?

10. Rapid Reproduction: No multiplying movements specialize in planting churches that will buy 20-plus acres, run four capital campaigns, and build three phases of a building before the church multiplies. Multiplying movements, from the house church variety to the more conventional congregations, typically encourage some sort of planting to emerge within a couple years. With United Methodists in the Philippines, a new faith community is not considered ready to begin weekly worship until it is ready to simultaneously adopt another neighborhood for mission outreach— meaning that they are beginning the planting of their offspring congregation at the same time that they are launching public worship. In most cases, leader development and spiritual formation will take 9 to 18 months before a new generation of ministries can be birthed. But when a group or ministry or church waits longer than two years to begin working toward the birth of the next thing, the chances are rising that they will settle in and never multiply rather than continue pioneering new frontiers. Jesus and his disciples never stayed in one place for long.

> What would change about your ministry if you started with replication in mind?

 **Hop to it!**

Take a few minutes to identify soil boosters that are evident in your congregation.

_____

_____

_____

_____

Jot down an idea or two that would help these elements gain real traction. For example, if prayer is evident, how can you make it more so? Perhaps you would sponsor a time of prayer and fasting for the entire congregation. You might do a churchwide study on prayer. Practice some new forms of spiritual listening. Take a group of folks on a prayer walk in your neighborhood.[5]

Or you may wish simply to immerse your church in a reconsideration of the life and experience of the early church. Get in touch with your roots as a spiritual movement, starting with the most ancient source material: the Book of Acts.[6]

_____

_____

_____

_____

3

Raise the Spiritual Temperature

One day, a dog noticed a rabbit. This dog was so fascinated by the rabbit that he started pursuing the rabbit; carefully creeping toward it until the rabbit bolted. As soon as that happened, the dog jumped, barked, and wagged his tail out of excitement and a chase ensued.

The rabbit kept darting back and forth as if they were playing tag. As the rabbit and dog left the dog's property and headed through town, they encountered a neighborhood with several dogs in it. Some of these dogs were lying down, some of them were drinking water, some of them were playing, and others were just observing.

Many of these dogs saw the dog run past them. Those observers wondered why that dog was so enthusiastic and filled with glee, so they too joined in the chase. They too were barking and running along with the first dog. Dogs who initially didn't respond to the dog running past them started thinking, "It seems I'm missing something. I should run too!" And soon everyone was running.

After a while, some of the dogs got tired of running and stopped. The numbers continued to decline until only the first dog was left running.

The other dogs had briefly and simply been imitating other excited dogs. But in a short time, their interest waned and they went home. Because they hadn't seen the rabbit. Since they did not have a personal encounter with the rabbit, they weren't motivated in the chase.

Multiply Your
Impact

There is a huge difference in spiritual intensity between people who know Jesus and are fascinated by him and those who are excited because someone else is excited. How many in our congregations have actually "seen the rabbit"?

"Never be lacking in zeal, but keep your spiritual fervor, serving the Lord." Romans 12:11 NIV

All great Christian movements are intense spiritually, marked by a significant God encounter through Jesus Christ. The people in such movements fall in love with God and surrender to the wondrous dream of what God is seeking to do in the world through human beings. A spiritual fire burns within their hearts and souls. Without such personal passion for Christ, we lack an adequate source of energy for vital and multiplying ministry.

The congregations Christie studied in the *Romans 12 Project* were clearly different than typical mainline congregations. At each onsite visit, those gathered did a timeline activity where they were asked to place major milestones above or below the line to represent high points, low points, and turning points. When they described high and low points in their history there were clear and consistent descriptions of how God was at work in the formation of the congregation and mention of times of prayer, discernment around major decisions, and a pronounced abundance of expectation. Each of the diverse congregations visited had strong intentionality around demonstrating and practicing spiritual disciplines as a body.

There are four meta-themes that emerge in our study of multiplying spiritual movements. Spiritual intensity is the first of the four—and we believe that it drives the other three. (The others are missional alignment, dynamic relationships, and cultural openness. We will explore each in the pages ahead.) If we go back to the beginning of the Book of Acts, we see that the whole thing starts when a small group of people experienced the presence and power of the Holy Spirit a few days after the resurrection of Jesus.

Spiritual intensity

is one of the four

meta themes that

emerged in our

study of multiplying

spiritual movements.

We believe that it

drives the other three.

There can be a fine line between spiritual intensity and spiritual insanity. Many wondered which side of that line John the Baptist was on . . . But intensity does not lead to insanity. In fact, true spiritual intensity will help a movement avoid divergence into weird, egocentric excess. When people encounter the risen Christ, they are always left with a passion, a fire burning deep within their souls. The intensity may look different in a New England Episcopal parish than it looks in a South American Pentecostal church, but you can find fire in both places.

> When people encounter the risen Christ, they are always left with a passion, a fire burning deep within their souls.

Characteristics of congregations with strong spiritual intensity include:

- Many people have an expectation of encountering the living Christ personally and/or in the congregation.

- Practicing spiritual disciplines (prayer, Bible study, fasting, Christian works, and so on) is an important part of life together.

- People are willing to take risks as an expression of their faith and trust in God.

- Leaders—paid and unpaid—demonstrate spiritual vitality.

While we can and should always work
to inspire spiritual intensity in the context
of worship services, the great churches
go further. Jesus did his best work not in
the synagogue, but in home gatherings,
camping trips, at the community watering
holes, by the lakeshore, and in the streets.
If your church isn't seeking to cultivate
spiritual life in more intimate and more down-
to-earth venues than your worship service,
you are probably not seeing
the kind of intensity in your
people that will fuel a
multiplying movement.

Practicing spiritual
disciplines individually
and with others leads
to increased spiritual
fuel and intensity.

41

Multiply Your
Impact

 **Hop to it!**

What would you do differently as a congregation if you wanted to raise the number of people who "saw the rabbit"?

_____

_____

_____

_____

Looking at the list of spiritual intensity characteristics, which are strengths of your congregation?

_____

_____

_____

_____

4

Keep the
Main Thing
the Main Thing

As they continued their travel, Jesus entered a village. A woman by the name of Martha welcomed him and made him feel quite at home. She had a sister, Mary, who sat before the Master, hanging on every word he said. But Martha was pulled away by all she had to do in the kitchen. Later, she stepped in, interrupting them. "Master, don't you care that my sister has abandoned the kitchen to me? Tell her to lend me a hand."

The Master said, "Martha, dear Martha, you're fussing far too much and getting yourself worked up over nothing. One thing only is essential, and Mary has chosen it—it's the main course, and won't be taken from her."

Luke 10:38–42, The Message

All over the world, one thing that most people have in common is that that they are really, really busy: busy working to survive, busy raising families, busy cooking or finding something to eat, and in some cases busy with an overly ambitious agenda for hobbies and personal development. Whether we are talking about Vietnamese rice farmers who have only five days off per year, or suburbanites in Marin County, California, who live to give their children all that money can buy, or the billions of people who are constantly scrambling to take care of their basic needs—food, shelter, safety: people are just busy—busier than ever! Multiplying movement churches know that they are working with a limited amount of time in most people's lives. So they had best be very careful about how they spend this limited time, and get to "the main course," as Jesus put it. There just is not much time to be wasted on anything that is not developing people as disciples of Jesus, who in turn make more disciples.

> Invest your time in developing people as disciples of Jesus.

Therefore, these churches consistently prioritize the investment of their resources (time, talent, treasure) according to their biblical vision and mission. Plans and major initiatives stem clearly from their understanding of their core purpose and a quest for fruitfulness. They are willing to let go of strategies that aren't bearing as much fruit. The more a church is willing to hyper-focus on a few critical functions that flow from its mission, the more likely that church will be missionally aligned. On the other hand, when churches try to do too much, it becomes easier for the tail to wag the dog—and in some cases for people to forget which part is the tail and which part the dog.

Alignment in the church usually feels more like cat herding than leading a marching band in perfect formation. The process of getting a group of church leaders to agree on what it looks like to organize the life of the church around making world-changing disciples for Jesus is often messy.

Alignment in the

church usually feels

more like cat herding

than leading a

marching band in

perfect formation.

Not only is it messy, it is ongoing work. Just like a car needs regular realignments, so does the church. When your church slows down in its ability to assimilate and disciple additional folks, an alignment is needed. When the debates get deadlocked or a crisis erupts (like shrinking revenue or loss of participants) it is a chance to rethink what business you are in, and to realign everything. If leaders patiently and prayerfully push through the stuck spots, then they will usually see the movement get unstuck and moving again.

> Stuck moments occur when we are staffing or restructuring for the church we used to be.

During Paul's nine years at Gulf Breeze, the church multiplied from three worship services on one campus to seven worship services at three locations. That represented a lot of change and several moments when they got stuck. The stuck moments occurred sometimes because they were staffing for the church they were two years before. Other times it was because they did not put enough energy into the most fruitful endeavors. Realignment became a regular and intermittent process in the journey from 1,000 to 2,400 worshippers each weekend. One of the core values that rose to the surface for them in those years was the fact that they had to do a few things really well, and not try to spread their resources too thin or on less important matters.

That is missional alignment. Keeping the main thing the main thing.

Characteristics of churches with strong missional alignment include:

- A clear understanding of their mandate to reach new people.

- Alignment to a clear direction.

- Good strategic thinking that is a regular part of leadership conversations.

- The ability to make decisions about resources based on priority as opposed to pleasing people or maintaining the status quo. Preference is the enemy of obedience.

- A shared sense of competency about the church's ability to start new ministries.

Churches with strong missional alignment have an almost relentless attitude toward evaluating their faithfulness. In those places it is common for there to be a major shift in ministry strategy or allocation of resources within the last two years. Because just as most cars cannot stay aligned for more than a few thousand miles—neither can most churches!

 **Hop to it!**

How is your church living out the Great Commission (to love as God loves) and Great Commandment (to invite everyone around us into the movement of loving as God loves)?

_____

_____

_____

_____

Are you making decisions that lead you to reach those who are not yet here? If a person from Mars (or from down the street) looked at the decisions your church has made recently, at the way you spend your money and the list of activities on your monthly calendar, what business would he say you are in?

_____

_____

_____

_____

5

Build Positive Relationships

Once upon a time two brothers, who lived on adjoining farms, fell into conflict. It was the first serious rift in 40 years of farming side by side. Up until then, they had shared machinery and traded labor and goods as needed without a problem.

Then the long collaboration fell apart. It began with a small misunderstanding that grew into a major disagreement. Finally it exploded into an exchange of bitter words followed by weeks of silence.

One morning there was a knock on the older brother's door. He opened it to find a man with a carpenter's toolbox.

"I'm looking for a few days' work," he said. "Perhaps you would have a few small jobs here and there I could help with?"

"Yes," said the older brother. "I do have a job for you. Look across the creek at that farm. That's my neighbor; in fact, it's my younger brother. Last week there was a meadow between us, but he took his bulldozer to the river levee and now there is a creek between us. Well, he may have done this to spite me, but I'll do him one better."See that pile of lumber by the barn? I want you to build me a fence—an eight-foot fence—so I won't need to see his place or his face anymore."

The carpenter said, "I think I understand the situation. Show me the nails and the post-hole digger, and I'll be able to do a job that pleases you."

The older brother had to go to town, so he helped the carpenter get the materials ready and then he was off for the day.

The carpenter worked hard all that day measuring, sawing, nailing. About sunset when the farmer returned, the carpenter had just finished his job.

The farmer's eyes opened wide and his jaw dropped. There was no fence there at all. It was a bridge—a bridge stretching from one side of the creek to the other! A fine piece of work, handrails and all. And the neighbor, his younger brother, was coming toward them, his arms outstretched. "You are quite a fellow to build this bridge after all I've said and done."

The two brothers stood at each end of the bridge, and then they met in the middle, taking each other's hand.

They turned to see the carpenter hoist his toolbox onto his shoulder.

"No, wait! Stay a few days. I've got a lot of other projects for you," said the older brother.

"I'd love to stay on," the carpenter said, "but I have many more bridges to build."

Author Unknown

Disciple making depends in large part on our relational skills—our relationship with God and with others. A church's people must develop good habits for leading others into a transformative relationship with God through Christ. Relationships with one another, with guests, with community. Relationships shaped and led by Gospel values. It's all about practicing Gospel community!

A couple years ago, Paul attended Christie's church as a worshipper one Sunday, unannounced. (Both of our churches are in Washington DC—both vibrant, and each quite different!) So Paul

> How are you practicing Gospel community?

found himself a white guy in a multicultural church that is a mix of mostly African Americans and folks from other countries. He reflects, "I must have looked like Nebraska had just come in the door and sat down." But during the next few minutes, half a dozen people went out of their way to come and chat with Paul, learn his name, ask a few questions about where he lived and so forth—not too invasive, but enough that he began

The churches with
healthy and dynamic
relationships look past
what's in it for them as
they relate to others.

to feel like he really belonged in the place. At the end of the service three of those persons came back by, and all three called him by his name. So some time later, Paul asked Christie, "Was there some committee running that operation—were there little name cards that they passed from one to another—or hidden cameras with an operator in a back room who radioed to an usher: *Lonely white guy on row six*?" Christie assured him that what he experienced simply arises from the DNA of Emory Church.

Most of the people who wander into most churches do not come with some ready-made value to the church in terms of a capacity for committee work or even the ability to donate much. The churches with healthy and dynamic relation-ships look past what's in it for them as they relate to others.

> I-thou relationships accept others as children of God.

Martin Buber distinguishes between *I-it* rela-tionships and *I-thou* relationships. The former would be a relationship with a car—some-thing that we use to get us where we want to go. But relate like that to your kids and you will have a very stressful family life. *I-thou* rela-tionships accept others as children of God, who exist for God's glory and not for ours—we relate to them with respect, and hopefully with a sense of the way that we are enriched simply in knowing them. Some churches really master the *I-thou* thing at every level! The people encounters in such churches leave folks feeling good about what just happened—whether in a ministry team meeting or in a ministry event in the neighborhood.

Characteristics of congregations with healthy, dynamic relationships:

- The practice of strong welcoming behaviors—more than a program, but a way of being with newcomers.

- A strong track record of bringing people from the outside into participation in the community of faith.

- Positive experience partnering with other leaders and groups.

- A culture of healthy teamwork and leader development—including healthy conflict-management skills.

 **Hop to it!**

Is your church an island in your community? Is it an island with an oasis (living water for all) or a cannibal (be careful—they will eat you alive) reputation?

_____

_____

_____

_____

Where do bridges need to be built and walls torn down?

_____

_____

_____

_____

6

Savor the Gift of Diversity

Giraffe had a new home built to his family's specifications. It was a wonderful house for giraffes, with soaring ceilings and tall doorways. High windows ensured maximum light and good views while protecting the family's privacy. Narrow hallways saved valuable space without compromising convenience.

The house won the National Giraffe Home of the Year Award. The owners were very proud.

One day Giraffe, working in his state-of-the-art wood shop in the basement, happened to look out of the window.

Coming down the street was Giraffe's old friend Elephant. Giraffe poked his head out the window and invited Elephant in.

Elephant was delighted; he liked Giraffe and looked forward to knowing him better. Besides, he wanted to see the wood shop. So he walked up to the basement door and waited for it to open.

"Come in; come in," said Giraffe. But immediately they encountered a problem. While Elephant could get his head in the door, he could go no farther.

"It's a good thing we made this door expandable to accommodate my wood shop equipment," Giraffe said. "Give me a minute while I take care of our problem." He removed some bolts and panels to let his friend in.

The two acquaintances were happily exchanging wood-working stories when Giraffe's wife leaned her head down the basement stairs and called to her husband. "Telephone, dear; it's your boss."

"I'd better take that upstairs in the den," Giraffe told Elephant. "Please make yourself at home; this may take a while."

After some time, Elephant thought to himself, "Maybe I'll join Giraffe upstairs," But as he started up the stairs, he heard the wood begin to crack. He jumped off and fell back against the wall. It too began to crumble. As he sat there disheveled and dismayed, Giraffe came down the stairs.

"What on earth is happening here?" Giraffe asked in amazement.

"I was trying to make myself at home," Elephant said.

Giraffe looked around and thought for a moment. "Okay, I see the problem. The doorway is too narrow. We'll have to make you smaller. There's an aerobics studio near here. If you'd take some classes there, we could get you down to size."

"Maybe," Elephant said, unconvinced.

"And the stairs are too weak to carry your weight," Giraffe continued. "If you took a ballet class at night, I'm sure we could get you light on your feet. I really hope you'll do it. I like having you here."

"Perhaps," Elephant said. "But to tell you the truth, I'm not sure a house designed for a giraffe will ever really work for an elephant, not unless there are some major changes."

R. Roosevelt Thomas[7]

What major changes does your church need to make in order to truly savor and welcome all from your community? Openness to others goes beyond tolerance of those who are not like you and into sharing life, sharing decision making, sharing of self. How big is your comfort zone? However big it is, cultural openness asks it to be bigger, deeper, and more significant so that space is made for those who are different, who are newer, who are younger (or older) than you.

> Openness to others goes beyond tolerance.

Multiplying churches often have a way of enabling people to sojourn with them long before the sojourners may buy into all the church's beliefs or lifestyle covenants. This ability to make gracious space for people who are different, even for the kinds of folks our mother did not want us playing with as children—it is sheer gold when combined with spiritual intensity in the congregation.

We live in an era now known for "culture wars." One might assume that conservative churches these days would have more trouble with cultural openness than more liberal churches. But not so quick to that conclusion! Cultural openness has almost nothing to do with political or theological leanings, or even with open-mindedness.

In one conservative East Tennessee congregation, we noticed that when they took the *Readiness 360* inventory they went over the top on strong cultural openness behaviors. One of the highest we ever saw! When we explored further, we discovered a church that collectively was living in an intense season of awareness of God's presence among them. When God is in the house, it is hard to be focused on what we don't like about someone else. Also, this church demonstrated a core passion that everyone might come to know Jesus. They had no time to judge people at their church, any more than they would spend time doing that at the grocery store. You go to the store to get food, and you expect to see all kinds of people there. And in this case, they believed we all go to church to seek Christ, and we should obviously expect all kinds of people there, people with all manner of stories, lifestyles, haircuts, and marital arrangements (or lack thereof). The other thing we noted about the East Tennessee congregation was that their worship attendance had jumped more than sixty percent in the preceding year. High spiritual intensity coupled with radical cultural openness equaled evangelistic wildfire.

> We all go to church to seek Christ, and we should obviously expect all kinds of people there.

Paul's church in DC is from the same denomination as the Tennessee congregation, but in a very different neighborhood. One might expect it to be a bastion of cultural openness in such a cosmopolitan setting with scores of languages spoken within a few blocks. However, a couple years ago when they planned to add a new worship community on Sunday evenings with contemporary Christian music, a few folks in the church became nervous. Someone feared such a service might attract Republicans. (As if the church were not already a mix of political

High spiritual intensity

coupled with radical

cultural openness equals

evangelistic wildfire

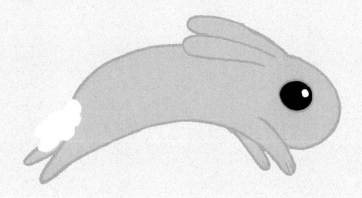

viewpoints.) Another said, "They might water down our values—we have worked to get this church just how we like it." The mission of the church prevailed, the service was launched, and now on Sunday nights, when they stand at the doors to greet people walking up the sidewalk, the gathered congregation is a close enough demographic snapshot of the people walking by that it is often impossible to predict who will turn and come in as they walk by and who will just walk on. The church people look like the community people—and so inside you discover multiple races, multiple income levels, single and couple, gay and straight, and (yes) Tea Party and liberals. All church, together!

This is cultural openness. It is made easier when a church clearly is able to claim that which unites them, and when a church is collectively aware of what God is doing in the place, it is so powerful that it cannot be threatened by anybody who walks in the door!

No church is going to hit a home run in every dimension of its life—and many churches in very homogeneous cultural regions will tend to be a little less developed in cultural openness naturally. But give the Holy Spirit some time and space to move around in a church, and it is amazing what happens!

Sometimes an overactive judging gene limits our ability to engage with others in constructive ways. Other times a fixation on certain social issues or values can get in the way of our loving people and leading them toward experiences of God's grace. In still other situations, we may have a knowing-doing gap; that what we understand or believe doesn't show up in our actions. In all cases, the best "gap-filling" occurs when God bestows on us so much love and grace that it just overflows us: so that our own experience of God distracts us from viewing those around us critically, plus we are just filled with God's love in the way we relate to those around us.

"Draw the circle wide, draw the circle wide
No one stands alone, we'll stand side by
side. Draw the circle wide, draw it wider
still. Let this be our song! No one stands
alone, standing side by side, draw the
circle wide!" ~ lyrics by Gordon Light

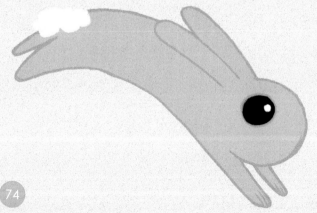

Characteristics of congregations with strong cultural openness include:

- A collection of attitudes and behaviors that support receptivity to folks who aren't like them.

- A good ability to form meaningful community with people who puzzle and/or offend you in certain respects.

- A perception that diversity in church is a good thing.

- Energy for working with different kinds of people.

- Willingness and ability to share power with new people.

- Valuable experiences that help them reach young people.

- Valuable experiences that help them reach people in their neighborhood that aren't like them.

 **Hop to it!**

Does your church reflect your community? At least some of the dominant people groups in terms of age, life situation, ethnicity, and/or socio-economic level?

_____

_____

_____

_____

What would it look like if you shared ownership of your church with those newer to Christianity and/or younger than you?

_____

_____

_____

7

Lead with
Your Strengths

Once upon a time the animals decided they must do something heroic to meet the problems of a "new world," so they organized a school. They had adopted an activity curriculum consisting of running, climbing, swimming, and flying. To make it easier to administer the curriculum, all the animals took all the subjects.

The duck was excellent in swimming. In fact, better than his instructor. But he made only passing grades in flying and was very poor in running. Since he was slow in running, he had to stay after school and also drop swimming in order to practice running. This was kept up until his webbed feet were badly worn and he was only average in swimming. But average was acceptable in school, so nobody worried about that, except the duck.

The rabbit started at the top of the class in running but had a nervous breakdown because of so much makeup work in swimming.

The squirrel was excellent in climbing until he developed

frustration in the flying class, where his teacher made him start from the ground up instead of the treetop down. He also developed leg cramps from overexertion and then got a C in climbing and a D in running.

The eagle was a problem child and was disciplined severely. In the climbing class, he beat all the others to the top of the tree but insisted on using his own way to get there.

At the end of the year, an abnormal eel that could swim exceedingly well and also run, climb, and fly a little had the highest average and was valedictorian.

The prairie dogs stayed out of school and fought the tax levy because the administration would not add digging and burrowing to the curriculum. They apprenticed their children to a badger and later joined the groundhogs and gophers to start a successful private school.

George Reavis,
former Assistant Superintendent of Cincinnati Public Schools

One of the distinguishing characteristics of the places that multiply is a strength-based approach to life. Too often congregations struggle for years to improve something they don't do well and get discouraged in the process. Filling potholes night and day is just not inspiring for most groups of people. If that same time was invested in strengths-based development, chances are they would be well on their way toward playing a better game.

> Just a little push might make all the difference in the world!

Imagine a bunch of golf balls scattered all over a golf course. Each ball represents a critical aspect of your church's ministry. Some balls are in the holes already—indicating that you are doing really well in those areas. Other balls are sitting on the green, near holes. Those balls just need a little putt or two and they will be in the hole. Other balls are in the woods, sand traps, and duck ponds. Every church has these too.

You could take your whole congregation into the duck pond en masse and divide into zones to find the ball. And still you might fail to even locate the ball, let alone get it in the hole. And even if you found the ball and you got it onto a green and into a hole—you will have expended massive energy to get one ball in one hole. With the same energy, your church could have hit in the half-dozen balls already within a putt of a hole. If you had taken the strengths-based approach, you would have addressed six areas of ministry functionality and developed your church's sense of competency at getting the job done. You also would have built up enough momentum to try a more difficult ball. This is how strengths-based development works.

Readiness 360 can help your congregation find and agree on the balls that are on the green. The places where relative strength already exists and just a little push might make all the difference in the world!

Sometimes (not always!) churches in the American heartland are made up of people who have limited life experience as friends and teammates with folks from other ethnic and cultural backgrounds. These churches may be less developed in their capacities for cultural openness than their cohorts in the urban coastal zones. But these same churches may excel in spiritual intensity and mission alignment. In the big cities, multicultural churches are on the increase these days, and yet with such diversity coming together, missional alignment may pose an extra challenge. And yet we see churches in all sorts of communities, and with all sorts of learning curves, thriving in both urban and rural/ex-urban areas when they play to their strengths—and when they grow their spiritual intensity in ways appropriate to their context.

Your church will never be good at everything.

Lead with what you are good at; build upon what you know how to do well.

Lead with
Your Strengths

And then, in terms of what is not as good as it needs to be, start with the areas where your effort is more likely to pay off with renewed ministry functionality. Often these are known as "quick wins." The more you follow these guidelines, the quicker the win will be.

Characteristics of congregations that lead with their strengths include:

- A glass-is-half-full attitude, celebrating the gifts and strengths they have as a church rather than fixating on the ways that they are deficient.

- A spirit of fun coming out in all sorts of ways and in all sorts of places.

- A reputation for excellence in a few things.

- And because such congregations often feel better about themselves, they tend to be more successful garnering time and financial commitments from participants.

 **Hop to it!**

Reflecting on your answers to the questions in topics 2–6, what are your church's strengths in these critical areas of ministry?

_____

_____

_____

_____

Identify some potential quick wins. Then pick the one that meets the criteria AND feels very close to a hole.

_____

_____

_____

_____

8

Be Nimble

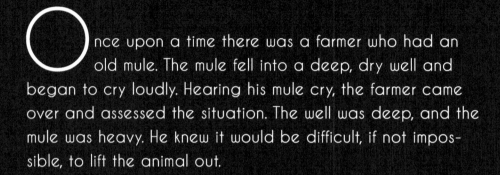

Once upon a time there was a farmer who had an old mule. The mule fell into a deep, dry well and began to cry loudly. Hearing his mule cry, the farmer came over and assessed the situation. The well was deep, and the mule was heavy. He knew it would be difficult, if not impossible, to lift the animal out.

Because the mule was old and the well was dry, the farmer decided to bury the animal in the well. In this way he could solve two problems: put the old mule out of her misery and have his well filled.

He called upon his neighbors to help him, and they agreed to help. To work they went. Shovelful of dirt after shovelful of dirt began to fall on the mule's back. She became hysterical.

Then all of a sudden an idea came to the mule. Each time they would throw a shovelful of dirt on her back, she could shake it off and step up. Shovelful after shovelful, the mule would shake it off and step up. Now exhausted and dirty, but quite alive, the mule stepped over the top of the well and walked through the crowd.

Anonymous

If the mule hadn't been focused (on getting out of the well) and flexible in her thinking, she would have been buried alive. If a faith community learns to roll with the punches—to shake it off and step up—it is much better able to continue on the path toward multiplying its impact. Yet too often churches can become consumed with focusing on who did what to whom that they don't even realize they are literally burying themselves— and their potential—alive.

> Too often churches can become consumed with who did what to whom.

Additionally, if the mule had not been struck with sudden inspiration, no amount of resolve would have gotten her out of the well.

We believe that churches most easily attain focus, flexibility, and resilience when they are intentionally focused on discerning God's call and leading in their corporate life. It takes inspiration from beyond our circle of familiar faces. Much has been written in recent years on how to get organizations and communities focused so they can pull together with synergy and move forward.

However, we have never seen a church find a sense of renewed focus without that church experiencing a renewed sense of God's call, a renewed sense of what God was saying to them, specifically and directly.

We would not wish upon any church another tedious sequence of meetings (too often in the Fellowship Hall on Tuesday evenings, sitting on cold metal chairs) where words are parsed and vision debated, until finally a document is produced that has too many words, that no one can remember, and that leaves us clueless as to what difference we are going to make in the world as a result of it!

We have also watched too many churches read good books, pull down detailed demographic reports, and even become experts in all the latest ministry tactics that worked five years ago at some church in Atlanta or Orlando—and to no avail! A little education about what's going on around us is a great thing—but it will not lead a diverse group of leaders easily to the right next steps for their ministry.

Even the tips that would come from a customized study of the church's core prac-tices (such as the *Readiness 360* otters) are

not enough. They will certainly be helpful to any church—but they will be infinitely more helpful when a church has taken some time to reflect in the presence of God about where God is calling them to go and what difference God is calling them to make in the world.

There is no substitute for a season of prayerful discernment. If we learn nothing else from the multiplying church, we should learn that the Book of Acts church prays, waits, listens, and then obeys when the Spirit blows. The Holy Spirit will be more helpful in getting your church focused and mobilized as one than all the organizational development visioning processes that you could run in the next 30 years.

Be Nimble

There is no substitute
for a season of
prayerful discernment

So stop for a season and pray. Slow down some of your church activity if necessary. Enter a season of discernment. Invite as many people as possible into this collective conversation with God. You might read the Book of Acts together as you proceed through this season, or perhaps one of the Gospels and Acts as a dual read. This kind of investment is always worth the time. Talk together about what it means to be a spiritual movement rather than simply an institution or a social/spiritual fraternity.

And then ask one another, "What is it that almost all of us are hearing together?" The significant aha moments may come first to one person in your group, who then shares what he or she is thinking and light bulbs go on all over the room—or it may be a group discovery where suddenly everyone just knows, just feels it, with a sense of clarity and unity.

Either way, the great thing about God's call, when it comes to a person or to your whole community: it is never too much, or too broad, or too vague, or too scattered. It is always just right, and always appropriately focused, always within your reach, and always clear in terms of what the next key steps we must take are.

And when we gain clarity about those next steps, it is absolutely, totally, critically, profoundly essential that . . . we act. Ultimately, it will be our church's move. We have to hop to it.

Characteristics of nimble congregations include:

- A sincere and humble dependency on God's leadership (as discerned by collective prayer) related to all major decisions.

- A willingness to experiment and try new things. When new things don't work, there isn't a sense of setback or any blame games.A sense of urgency to try and a lack of anxiety about failing.

- A grounding in something deeper other than outward habit and routine, so that even as practices change, something deeper gives stability.

The great thing about
God's call: it is never
too much, or too
broad, or too vague,
or too scattered. It
is always just right.

 ## Hop to it!

What simple thing does your church need to do now in order to be a focused, nimble listener?

_____

_____

_____

_____

Multiply Your
Impact

End Notes

1 http://www.youtube.com/watch?v=jAoqdBDL5_g.

2 http://www.cmaresources.org/article/secret-to-church-multiplication-movements

3 For more about the principle of "good enough," see Dave Browning's book, *Deliberate Simplicity*, Zondervan 2009.

4 *Seven Practices of Effective Ministry* by Andy Stanley, Reggie Joiner and Lane Jones, pg 101

5 *A Prayer Walk Guide* by Cheri Holdridge is available for free download at http://www.epicentergroup.org/#/cultural-relevance/community-listening-tools. Scroll to the bottom of the page for the link.

6 *Catch Fire in 50 Days* is a book designed for groups of leaders and Christians reading, reflecting, praying, and responding to the Book of Acts over a fifty-day period of time. There are free downloadable sermon series outlines and small-group templates as well. It is available for purchase in bulk at www.readiness360.org.

7 *Building a House for Diversity*, by R. Roosevelt Thomas Jr. New York: American Management Association, 1999, pp. 3–5.

CPSIA information can be obtained
at www.ICGtesting.com
Printed in the USA
LVOW06s1000180916
505123LV00034B/162/P